As Far As the Eye Can Reach

Lewis and Clark's Westward Quest

As Far As the Eye Can Reach

Lewis and Clark's Westward Quest

ELIZABETH CODY KIMMEL

Landmark Books®

Random House New York

www.randomhouse.com/kids

Library of Congress Cataloging-in-Publication Data
Kimmel, Elizabeth Cody.
As far as the eye can reach : Lewis and Clark's westward quest / Elizabeth Cody Kimmel.
p.   cm. — (Landmark books)
Summary: An account of the journey across the unexplored territory west of the
Mississippi River undertaken by Meriwether Lewis and William Clark in the early
eighteen hundreds by order of President Jefferson.
ISBN 0-375-81348-9 (trade) — ISBN 0-375-91348-3 (lib. bdg.)
1. Lewis and Clark Expedition (1804–1806)—Juvenile literature.
2. West (U.S.)—Discovery and exploration—Juvenile literature.
3. West (U.S.)—Description and travel—Juvenile literature. [1. Lewis and Clark
Expedition (1804–1806). 2. West (U.S.)—Discovery and exploration.] I. Title.
F592.7 .K547 2003
917.804'2—dc21   2002031621

Printed in the United States of America
10 9 8 7 6 5 4 3 2 1
First Edition

RANDOM HOUSE and colophon and LANDMARK BOOKS and colophon are registered
trademarks of Random House, Inc.

Photo credits are found on page 113.

For Jean Kimmel,
with love and affection
—E.C.K.

Special thanks to James J. Holmberg of
the Filson Club Historical Society
in Louisville, Kentucky

Contents

Prologue

$\mathcal{A}$t last, an Indian! The sight left Meriwether Lewis weak with relief. He and his men had traveled over two thousand miles across the wild continent of North America. Never had they been more tired, more broken-down, and more in need of help than now.

The Indian was a Shoshone. Lewis could trade with the Shoshone for the horses he needed so badly to get his men over the mountains. There was no time to waste. It was late summer, and the nights were already turning cold. If they were to cross the

The heavy black line shows Lewis and Clark's journey from St. Louis to the Pacific Ocean. The second line through Montana follows the different route taken on their return trip.

mountains before the first of the winter snows blocked the passes, they must go right away. Without horses, their chance of success was nearly impossible.

Lewis's orders—to follow the Missouri River to its source and continue to the western coast of the continent—came from no less than the president

EW YORK

YLVANIA

GINIA

of the United States himself. It was 1805, and the U.S. was just twenty-nine years old. President Thomas Jefferson had placed his hopes for the future of the young country to Lewis and the expedition's co-commander, William Clark.

By completing their journey, Lewis and Clark would create a firm claim on all the territory they passed through. These claims would greatly expand American trade possibilities in the west, where the British were already trapping and trading valuable furs. And a river route to the Pacific Ocean would make shipping furs to Asia much easier and less costly.

More importantly, a successful trip would help stop the spread of other countries' land claims in North America. Already the British had forts in the north, providing protection for British trappers in the area. Even the existence of these forts was a step toward Britain claiming the territory as their own. Native Americans, of course, had occupied these lands for hundreds of years. And the Spanish and Russians also had designs on the continent.

It was a crucial time for American land expansion. The government needed a legitimate claim on the vast tracts of land that stretched thousands of miles west of the colonies. Lewis and Clark's expedition could provide that claim, if they succeeded in reaching the west coast. But first they needed to cross the Rockies, and Lewis could not do that without the help of the Shoshone and their horses.

Lewis and Clark had been searching for the Shoshone for weeks. The men in the expedition were exhausted, and Clark himself was ill. While Clark's party continued upriver, Lewis had taken a party of three men on foot to continue the search. And now they had found what they were looking for.

The men and the Indian began cautiously to approach one another. Lewis had come carrying a blanket filled with gifts. He halted and opened the blanket on the grass to display its contents. Two of Lewis's men stopped, but one man missed his discreet signal and continued moving forward. That was all it took to break the mood of cautious trust. Turning his horse around, the Indian galloped away. In moments he was swallowed up by the mountainous landscape. Lewis and his men were alone again.

Had they just missed their last chance?

Chapter One

Capt. Lewis is brave, prudent, habituated to the woods, & familiar with Indian manners & character. He is not regularly educated, but he possesses a great mass of accurate observation on all the subjects of nature which present themselves here, & will therefore readily select those only in his new route which shall be new.

THOMAS JEFFERSON, LETTER TO DR. BENJAMIN RUSH, FEBRUARY 28, 1803

*F*or years President Jefferson had dreamed of a cross-country expedition to the Pacific Ocean. Now it was 1803, and his dream was finally becoming reality. Jefferson gave the dream a name—the Corps of Discovery. It would be the most important journey made in the history of the country, and the president took it very seriously. The potential for geographic and scientific discoveries seemed unlimited. And Jefferson believed that if the United States was the first to find and map a water route to the Pacific, called the Northwest Passage, they would

The artist Charles Peale painted this portrait of Meriwether Lewis. Mr. Peale also ran the museum in Philadelphia that displayed many of the items collected by the Corps on its expedition.

not only make a discovery of enormous importance, but would come closer to gaining control of the entire continent.

Jefferson had little difficulty choosing a man to lead the Corps of Discovery. Meriwether Lewis was an ambitious and intellectually curious young man who had spent his Virginia childhood learning the names of every plant and animal he came across. When he was only eighteen, Lewis was already running his family's two-thousand-acre plantation. It was his first taste of responsibility, and he proved to be a reliable and effective leader.

By 1803 Lewis had already traveled extensively, including a lengthy journey on the Ohio River. He had served as a captain in the army, and when Jefferson began organizing the expedition, Lewis was working as the president's personal secretary.

Jefferson had great faith in the twenty-eight-year-old Lewis. Lewis knew a good deal about the land, about Indians, and about plants and animals. Jefferson made sure Lewis was taught what he did not already know. He sent his secretary to an assortment of experts who schooled him in everything from the science of fossils to the basics of emergency medical treatment.

As the expedition plans progressed, a historic event took place. In the beginning of 1803, the territory that made up the United States of America extended no farther west than the Mississippi River. The enormous area of land just to the west of American territory was a possession of France.

The French emperor, Napoleon Bonaparte, needed to raise money for his army. He made an unexpected offer to sell the land, called the Louisiana Territory, to the Americans. In one simple sale, for the price of 15 million dollars, or three cents an acre, the United States of America grew over 800,000 square miles larger. The country was suddenly twice its former size.

The United States now claimed ownership of over half the continent, making the Corps of Discovery even more important. Although the rough outline of the Louisiana Territory had been mapped, very little was known about the land America had just bought. However, there was no

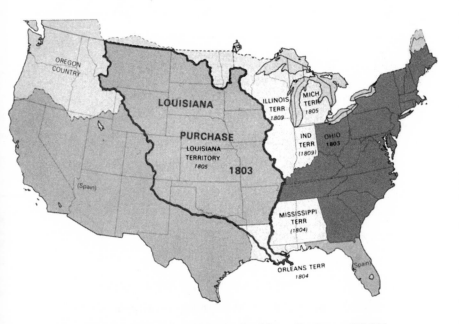

Purchased from France in 1803, the Louisiana Territory, 828,000 square miles of land west of the Mississippi River, doubled the size of the United States.

shortage of stories, and President Jefferson himself believed some of them.

People told tales of a race of tiny cannibals, of a salt mountain, of herds of woolly mammoths, and of volcanoes erupting with lava. Many believed a lost tribe of Welshmen, who had come to North America from Great Britain centuries before, lived in the heart of the territory. Traders had some contact with the Indians who lived along the closest section of the Missouri River, but no one really knew what the land contained or whether the Indians living farther north and west were fierce or friendly. Jefferson left it to Lewis to find out.

It was going to be a long, difficult journey, and it was extremely important that the Corps have more than enough supplies. This required Jefferson and Lewis to do a great deal of planning ahead, trying to foresee the men's needs on the journey. Obviously they needed large quantities of food, which they would supplement by hunting and fishing. Weapons and sturdy clothing were crucial. And many of the Indian tribes the expedition expected to meet would have never come across white people before. Making a good first impression would be important.

Winning the favor and trust of the Indian tribes was a vital part of the Corps' trip. Jefferson would need to keep things peaceful in the new

This document lists the presents Lewis purchased to give to the Native Americans the Corps expected to meet on its journey. He includes 30 calico shirts, 12 red silk handkerchiefs, and 288 knives.

American territory of the Louisiana Purchase. And in order to make the most of the trading opportunities across the continent, the Americans would have to be on friendly terms with the native people living there.

Lewis did not want to head the expedition alone. And he knew right away who he wanted to help him lead it. William Clark had once been Lewis's commanding officer in the Army. Like Lewis, Clark was Virginia-born. He had moved to Louisville, Kentucky, at fourteen, spent many years living on the frontier, and was very familiar with life in the

William Clark posed for this portrait around 1810, after his return from the journey of discovery. The portrait, like the one of Meriwether Lewis earlier in this chapter, is by the artist Charles Peale.

wild. He was strong, resourceful, and had experience with Indians. Most importantly, Lewis liked and trusted him. Clark eagerly accepted Lewis's offer to co-command the Corps.

What remained now was to recruit the right kind of men to form the rest of the group. In Louisville, William Clark received dozens of inquiries and applications from men eager to join the Corps of Discovery. Lewis was in Pittsburgh overseeing the building of the keelboat for the expedition, and he, too, was swamped with requests to join up. Word had spread fast, and it was clear that the Corps of Discovery was undertaking one of the greatest journeys in American history. Many men wanted to take part.

With so many to choose from, Lewis and Clark were able to pick only the applicants with the very highest qualifications. Each needed to know the land, to be familiar with river travel, to be a skilled hunter and tracker. They needed to be reliable and physically strong. They must be comfortable in the rough and unknown wilderness.

Over thirty-five were chosen, including a slave of Clark's named York, who was a brave and trustworthy man.

Finally everything was in place. It was August of 1803. Lewis watched the last nail being hammered into the keelboat, then began loading his supplies. Before long, he was sailing down the Ohio River in the direction of Louisville, Kentucky, where he would meet up with Clark and the men they had selected for the Corps. At last Lewis was on the move.

Chapter Two

Set out at half passed three oClock under three Cheers
from the gentlemen on the bank and proceeded on to the
head of the Island . . . Soon after we Set out to day a
hard Wind from the W.SW accompanied with a hard
rain, which lasted with Short intervales all night.

JOURNAL OF WILLIAM CLARK, MAY 21, 1804

*B*ut Captain Lewis did not keep moving for long.
He had no intention of trying to go up the Missouri
River before the winter of 1803–04. Once he and
Clark agreed on who they would hire for the Corps,
the group traveled from Kentucky to Illinois, where
they built their winter quarters at Wood River.
It would be a long four-month layover, but it was
necessary. No journey west could start in the winter, when bitter cold and snows swept across the
land and the Missouri River froze over. Their

quarters built, the men settled down to wait for spring.

By April of 1804, the men were eager to be on the way. The weather had turned warmer, but Lewis was seeing to last-minute details and buying provisions in St. Louis. The expedition's departure was put off for another month. At last, on May 14, despite a steady rainfall, the Corps of Discovery started on its way.

Clark and his men met up with Lewis twenty-three miles upriver in St. Charles. Now the entire party was together—including the twenty-five enlisted men of the permanent party, the French Canadian interpreter George Drouillard, nine French boatmen to help with the boats, Clark's slave York, and the seven enlisted men who would accompany the Corps until it reached its winter quarters. Also with Lewis was his Newfoundland dog, Seaman.

With high spirits, the men boarded the boats and began up the Missouri River. They stopped at a few inhabited river villages before truly finding

Lewis's dog, Seaman, who accompanied the Corps on its journey, was a Newfoundland, like the one pictured in this etching.

themselves in the wild. From those villagers they received valuable information about the conditions the Corps would find as they headed upriver.

The expedition had three boats altogether. Two were open boats called pirogues. The third, called a keelboat, was much larger and considered the most important vessel of the expedition. The keelboat was fifty-five feet long and designed especially for the varied conditions on the Missouri

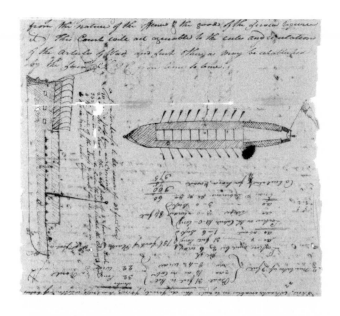

This entry in William Clark's journal shows his drawing of the keelboat. It was fifty-five feet long and had a mast that was thirty-two feet high.

River. It held up to twelve tons of supplies and could be sailed, rowed, poled, or even pulled along the river if needed. In many ways, the success of the boat design was key to the success of the expedition itself. If the boat couldn't make it up the river, the Corps of Discovery wouldn't either.

Their course followed the upriver path of the Missouri River, which ran from the east border to the west border of Missouri. The path of the river then turned northwest and touched the borders of present Kansas and Nebraska on the west, and present Iowa on the east. The river was unpredictable, and the boat's progress often slowed or stopped.

Unseen sandbars, submerged logs, and areas of rapidly surging water needed to be avoided. Sometimes Lewis decided to row around the obstacle or to thrust poles into the riverbed like crutches to push the boat slowly along. Other times he suggested the least popular solution—that the men hop out of the boat and wade along the shore, pulling the boat behind them with ropes. Every problem was made worse by the current, which flowed downriver against them. Even when the way was clear enough to use the sail, moving against the current was a constant battle.

The work was backbreaking and the sun relentless. Mosquitoes constantly tortured the men. Ticks buried themselves in their skin. Snakes bit their legs. Muscles strained and bones ached from the labor. And yet the men were getting what they had come for. They were traveling through country that only a handful of Americans had set eyes on. And before long, they would pass beyond the range of even the hardiest traders and trappers. No one knew what lay ahead. It was frightening and exciting. In short, to the Corps of Discovery, the adventure was worth every bit of the suffering.

By the end of June, the party had reached a bend in the Missouri River, near the mouth of the Kansas River. Here the Missouri began to angle to the north. Summer was upon them, with smothering hot days and violent thunderstorms.

Clark's journal noted that several men had become sick with dysentery. Others were suffering the effects of the overwhelming heat and humidity, coupled with the fatigue from hours of physical labor they performed every day. They were all exhausted. The smallest pests could be the worst, and often worthy of a journal mention. "The Ticks & Musquiters are verry troublesome," Clark wrote on June 17, with his customary departure from standard spelling.

The expedition had no doctor with them. On President Jefferson's recommendation, Lewis had visited at length with a physician before leaving, learning all he could about the most current theories of medical care. The physician, Dr. Rush, schooled Lewis carefully and organized a chest for Lewis containing all the supplies necessary in case of an emergency. Much of the information and medicine Lewis received, however, was of doubtful value. For example, Dr. Rush advised that the men eat very little on long and difficult marches. Dr. Rush also believed that bloodletting—making litle cuts in the skin and allowing a person to bleed— would release sickness from the body. And the cure-all medicine of choice was Dr. Rush's own invention—a pill that did little more than cause the taker to go to the bathroom

Like Dr. Benjamin Rush, many doctors believed that certain illnesses were best treated by bleeding a patient. George Washington, in fact, died in 1799 from a throat infection after being bled too much.

immediately. If Dr. Rush's remedies did not help much, fortunately they probably did not do much harm either.

Though the Corps' most essential goal was to find and map a route to the Pacific Ocean, President Jefferson also wanted them to make friends with the Indians along the way. Since the route the Corps was mapping would be used by American fur traders and trappers in the future, it was important to pave the way with a message of peace, and to encourage the Indians to trade with Americans. Lewis had expected to encounter the Kansas Indians near the Kansas River, but when the Corps passed by, he found the tribe had moved out onto the plains to hunt buffalo. The expedition would have to keep traveling upriver and be patient.

Although some days were slow going, on others the boats made very good progress. After a particularly good afternoon when records show they advanced fifteen miles upriver, the expedition had another stroke of good fortune. One of the men went hunting on the plains and came upon a

Missouri Indian. The man learned that though most of the tribe was away on a bison hunt, there was a group camped not too far off. Right away, Lewis issued an invitation for a council, or meeting.

Because of the importance of winning the Indians' favor, Lewis had brought many items intended to be given as gifts to the tribes. The gifts were meant both to please and honor the Indians, and to establish an American presence in their territory. Special medals had been made with the image of President Jefferson on one side and two hands shaking on the other. Other gifts included tobacco, mirrors, ivory combs, sewing needles, knives, paint, and army coats and hats.

Lewis and Clark gave peace medals to the Indians they came across. The clasped hands symbolize the friendship the explorers hoped to forge with the Indian tribes.

The council took place on August 3. The men of the Corps prepared some gifts for the Indians, as Clark wrote in his journal with his usual inventive spelling: "Mad up a Small preasent for those people . . . also a package with a Meadle [medal] to accompany a Speech for the Grand Chief." Clark's journal goes on to describe the meeting. The proposed speeches were given, and gifts of cloth, whiskey, and the "Meadle" were presented. The site became known as Council Bluffs. Lewis was very happy that their first meeting with Indians had gone

Sergeant Patrick Gass, a member of the expedition, kept a journal of the trip, which was first published in 1807. This illustration from the 1810 edition of the journal shows a meeting between an Indian tribe and Lewis and Clark.

well. Unfortunately, their string of good luck was about to run out.

Sergeant Charles Floyd had been complaining on and off of stomach pains. Because the men drank the murky river water, many of them had developed problems in their digestive tracts. Floyd, however, became sicker than anyone else. And his problem was more serious than any brought on by drinking water. As his condition weakened, it was clear that nothing was helping. On August 20, Sergeant Floyd died from what probably was a ruptured appendix. The death was hard on everyone, particularly Lewis and Clark. It reminded them of their growing isolation from civilization and of the danger that each one of them would be facing. They had been under way only three months before losing a man. How many more might be lost during the next year?

The men made Floyd a tidy grave on a hill and crafted a headstone from wood. There was nothing left to do but pack up and resume their journey toward the Pacific Ocean.

Chapter Three

*. . . the 2nd Chief was verry insolent both in words &
justures declareing I should not go on, Stateing he had
not receved presents sufficent from us, his justures were
of Such a personal nature I felt My self Compeled to
Draw my Sword—at this Motion Capt. Lewis ordered all
under arms in the boat . . .*

JOURNAL OF WILLIAM CLARK, SEPTEMBER 25, 1804

*B*y mid-September the Corps was traveling through
the Great Plains, one of the largest grasslands in
the world. It was flat and seemed endless. The green
and gold wind-whipped grass extended as far as the
eye could see. Most of the men on the expedition
had been born and raised in the woods of Kentucky,
Virginia, Pennsylvania, or other states along the
east coast. They had probably never laid eyes on
such an ocean-sized plot of open, treeless land.
Even after days of traveling through the prairie, the
sight must have amazed them.

Toward the end of the month, the expedition came upon three Indian boys swimming, and from them learned that a band of Teton Sioux were camped nearby. Lewis lost no time giving the boys some gifts of tobacco and asking them to set up a meeting with their elders the next day. The Corps had already met with a group of Yankton Sioux a few weeks earlier. That tribe had seemed very friendly. By all accounts, this was not going to be the case with the Teton Sioux.

In his extensive preparations for the journey, Lewis had learned enough about the Teton Sioux to make him both very cautious and very determined to have a successful council with them. They were a warlike and very powerful tribe. American and French traders from St. Louis who tried to go up the Missouri River were stopped by the Sioux over and over again. The traders were forced to part with their furs or goods for extremely low prices. British traders, on the other hand, were more often allowed to pass and were dealt with on much better terms.

This treatment suggested an allegiance between the Teton Sioux and the British, and President Jefferson considered it a serious threat to American trade. The Sioux must be persuaded that the Americans were the authority in this territory and would make the better trade partners. To do this, a positive relationship had to be created. The only people in a position to do this were Lewis and Clark.

The meeting began as planned on the morning of September 25, on a sandbar that formed a small island near the joining of the Missouri with the Bad River. Lewis started out as he had with the other tribes. He handed out gifts, gave speeches, and raised the American flag. A large number of Sioux warriors attended, including three chiefs: Black Buffalo, the Partisan, and Buffalo Medicine. On the banks, other Sioux, including women and children, gathered to watch. Lewis presented as gifts an army coat, hat, and several medals, and his men fired their guns into the air. The Sioux were far from impressed. Adding further to their problems, Lewis

Wahktageli, a Yankton Sioux chief, posed for the painter Karl Bodmer in 1833. Around his neck hangs one of the large peace medals given to Indians by Lewis and Clark.

had left their Sioux-language interpreter back with the Yankton Sioux to arrange for some of them to visit Washington. Communication was very difficult. The only thing that could be understood was the Sioux's unhappiness with the gifts they had been given. They were not enough. The Sioux wanted more, much more.

In an attempt to keep the peace, Lewis and Clark invited the chiefs on board the keelboat and offered them whiskey to drink. Afterward, Clark organized a party of several men to escort the chiefs back to shore in one of the small pirogues. Now the trouble began in earnest. On reaching the shore, three Sioux warriors got out and took hold of the rope attached to the pirogue's bow. Another warrior grabbed the boat's mast. One of the chiefs deliberately stumbled against Clark in a threatening manner, demanding more gifts before he would leave. In the small boat, Clark and his seven men were greatly outnumbered. He was surrounded by the Sioux, and the mood was quickly becoming more and more hostile. Feeling he must now make a show of force, Clark pulled his sword out of its scabbard.

Lewis, watching from the keelboat, immediately ordered his men to ready their weapons. In addition to rifles, muskets, and pistols, the keelboat carried a small cannon. Within moments, the guns were pointed at the Sioux warriors, and Lewis held a lit match an inch from the cannon's fuse. On the shore, the Sioux pointed their own weapons, arrows and guns, at the keelboat.

The chief, Black Buffalo, suddenly broke the standoff by grabbing the pirogue's bow rope and ordering the warriors to stand aside. Perhaps he wished to avoid a bloodbath, or maybe his was simply a cooler head prevailing. Clark was able to row the pirogue away from the shore and back to the keelboat. Black Buffalo and several of his men waded through the water and asked to spend the night on board the keelboat. Lewis and Clark agreed, and what might have been a deadly battle ended with a tense but uneventful overnight visit. Clark explained in his journal that night that "I call this Island bad humered Island as we were in a bad humer."

The next morning Black Buffalo asked Lewis to come with him to his village. Though shaken by the near-battle the day before, Lewis was still determined to make a good relationship with the Teton Sioux. He therefore accepted the invitation. Later, Clark and most of the Corps members joined him there.

Close to one thousand Sioux lived in the village, which was made up of a grouping of one hundred tepees. Black Buffalo planned a feast and a campfire dance for his visitors. The men of the Corps welcomed the feast of roasted buffalo meat, but the Scalp Dance performed by the women reminded them that the Sioux were a warlike people. Throughout the evening, everyone in the expedition remained carefully on their guard. Some prisoners, members of the Omaha tribe, whispered that the Teton Sioux planned to assault and rob the expedition members. Though the attack never came, the men's nervousness increased.

The following evening Black Buffalo held a second feast and Scalp Dance. In spite of the festivities, the expedition members and the Indians grew more and more distrustful of one another. There were several misunderstandings and close calls. By the time the keelboat departed the next morning, more sharp words had been exchanged. Lewis must have felt a mixture of relief and disappointment as they continued upriver, leaving the Teton Sioux

Tepees, used as housing by many Plains Indian tribes, are shown here in *Sioux Camp*, painted by Karl Bodmer around 1833.

village behind. They had avoided a fight, it was true, but they had also failed to start the friendly relationship that President Jefferson wanted.

They were now in the area of present-day Pierre, South Dakota. The weather was beginning to turn cold. Though each day brought them slightly closer to their ultimate goal of the Pacific Ocean, Lewis had never planned for the Corps to travel during the coldest months. Soon it would be time to stop the expedition for the winter and build a camp. As they made their way north, the expedition passed a series of abandoned earthen lodges. The lodges had once been lived in by members of the Arikara tribe, who had controlled the Missouri River in this area. Their people had numbered in the tens of thousands until smallpox, accidentally introduced by white trappers and traders, had all but destroyed their population. Lewis and Clark met with a village of the survivors. The meeting was quite the opposite of what they had gone through with the Teton Sioux.

The Arikara were open, friendly, and seemed

eager to form a good relationship with these men who represented President Jefferson, the Great Father. They accepted the Corps' gifts, although they refused the whiskey the men offered to share with them. Lewis was also pleased to find that a trader, Joseph Gravelines, had been living in the village for fifteen years. Now they would have none of the difficulty in communicating and translating that they had experienced with the Teton Sioux.

The greatest success of the visit, however, was York. Never having seen a black-skinned man before, the Arikara were fascinated and enchanted by him, and even the village children wanted York to play with them. Clark wrote that "many came to view us all day, much astonished at my black Servent, who did not lose the opportunity of [displaying] his powers Strength &c." Everyone wanted to talk to or touch York. They called him the Big Medicine.

As the only black man on the expedition, York is certainly a historic figure. And yet very little is known about him. Over time, many stories have

A mural painted by E. S. Paxson in 1912, *Lewis and Clark at Three Forks,* includes this detail of York, Clark's slave.

circulated about him, some claiming he had supernatural strength, others that he was a buffoon and the main comic relief of the Corps. His name appears from time to time in expedition journals, but for the most part he remains a silent participant. We know he often went with Clark to hunt game. We also know that when York became sick, Clark treated him. But whether or not he enjoyed being on the expedition—and what his feelings were when examined and exclaimed over by the Indians—remains a mystery we can only speculate about.

After a visit of several days, it was time for the Corps of Discovery to move on. Lewis was satisfied with the Arikara's promises of peaceful intentions, though he could not protect them against war from other tribes as they asked. For the time being, it was enough that the visit had gone peacefully. With the trader Gravelines joining them, they continued upriver in the direction of the Mandan villages.

If the Mandan did not turn out to be as welcoming as the Arikara, it was going to be a long winter.

Chapter Four

Weather is So Cold that we do not think it prudent to turn out to hunt in Such Cold weather, or at least untill our Consts. are prepared to go under this Climate. I measure the river from bank to bank on the ice and make it 500 yards.

JOURNAL OF WILLIAM CLARK, DECEMBER 12, 1804

$\mathcal{T}$he Mandan appeared on the riverbanks to greet the Corps of Discovery, and based on this friendly reception, Lewis felt hopeful that his men could safely winter near their villages. The Mandan had often been visited by both Indian and white traders, and they welcomed the new opportunities that the expedition would bring.

Now Lewis and Clark investigated the land on foot. They would need to find a suitable site to spend the entire winter, before the snows came and the river froze over. They would not be able to continue toward the Pacific Ocean until spring, when the river again became navigable.

They soon found a good place for their winter quarters. The men worked as quickly as possible to complete the compound, which was made up of a series of small cabins and a storage building. The

This illustration from the journal of expedition member Patrick Gass shows members of the Corps building Fort Mandan, where they would spend the winter of 1804–05.

entire site was surrounded by a triangular eighteen-foot-high wall. Fort Mandan, named after the Indian tribe, was finished with little time to spare. Temperatures had dropped from pleasantly chilly to dangerously cold in just a few weeks, and the winter promised to be a harsh one. On November 13, Clark noted in his journal that it had "Snow'd all day, the Ice ran thick and air Cold."

The Corps found their new Indian neighbors to be generous and very helpful. Building the winter camp was quite hard work, and the men needed a great deal of fresh meat to eat every day. The Mandan held a ceremony to call a herd of buffalo to be hunted. Several days later, when the herd did appear, the Mandans shared the information with Lewis and Clark, and the two groups hunted together.

In turn, one of Lewis's men set up a small forge and made and repaired tools and weapons for the Mandan. For these services, the expedition was able to trade for more food, such as corn, beans, and squash. The two groups began to pay friendly visits to each other as the temperature grew even colder and the winter set in. On November 29, Clark noted that "the depth of the Snow is various in the wood about 13 inches. The river Closed [frozen over] at the Village above." This made the halt in their journey official—the Corps could not leave until the river thawed in the spring.

At last Lewis and Clark had a lengthy opportunity to observe and learn about a group of Indians. Their previous encounters with the Sioux and other tribes had been rushed and consisted mostly of gift giving and attempts to curry favor. But President Jefferson had instructed Lewis to learn as much as possible about Indians. Now they had months of winter to pass before resuming their western journey, and this gave them the chance to get to know the Mandan, to study firsthand their customs and way of life . . . perhaps even to become true friends.

The Mandan, along with three neighboring villages of Hidatsa, lived in round, dome-roofed earthen lodges. Each lodge was large enough to house several families, stockpiles of food, and sometimes even a few horses. Together the Hidatsa and Mandan totaled about four thousand people. The Mandan were farmers and hunters, both growing vegetables and sending parties out on horseback for

This pictograph is by Sitting Rabbit, a member of the Mandan tribe. The domed lodges of the Mandan villages of the Knife River were typical of the Mandan and Hidatsa tribes.

buffalo and other game. They were also traders, exchanging items with other tribes and with French Canadian and British trappers.

Two French Canadians were living among the Mandan. One, named René Jusseaume, agreed to work for Lewis during the winter as an interpreter and instructor in the Mandan ways. The second man, named Toussaint Charbonneau, agreed to join the expedition when it continued west, as long as his wife could come along. She was a young, pregnant Shoshone woman named Sacagawea. She had been taken prisoner by the Hidatsa tribe as a young girl, and she had not returned to her home since that time.

When the time came for the Corps to leave the village and proceed on its journey, they would seek out the Shoshone people. Hopefully these Shoshone would trade them their horses to help the Corps cross the mountains Lewis expected to find there. The Mandan had told them that horses were crucial to the crossing. Lewis knew that having a Shoshone woman in their party could be very helpful. Not only would Sacagawea be able to communicate with her people, but she might know some of the territory as well. Therefore, Lewis had a special interest in Sacagawea. When Sacagawea went into a difficult labor, Lewis heard about it and went to see what help he might give.

Actually, Lewis was no more qualified to help in childbirth than anyone else in the party. Certainly the medical lessons given him by Dr. Rush had not included how to deliver a baby. So when Jusseaume mentioned that he had heard crushed rattlesnake rings sometimes helped, Lewis quickly mixed up the potion from his own supplies. Within ten minutes of taking the mixture, Sacagawea gave birth to a healthy baby boy. Lewis privately recorded in his journal his doubts that the potion had really done anything, but the important thing was that mother and infant were both healthy. The child was named Jean Baptiste, and the Corps gave him the nickname of Pompy.

Fort Mandan stuck to a regular military schedule, with a posting of guards, inspections, and regular drills. But there was also free time for everyone. The men of the Corps made many visits to the Mandan lodges. Made of earth, timber, and grass, the lodges had a central smoke hole in the roof and were quite warm and comfortable dwellings. Lewis, Clark, and their men would sit with the Mandan late into the night, talking, eating, and dancing. The Mandan had drums and tambourines, and one of the men in the Corps was a fiddle player. They shared stories and songs. Of great importance was the information the Mandan gave on the land that lay to the west. Very little was known to Lewis and Clark about this area, present-day Montana. They listened eagerly as the Mandan hunters described the country.

Lewis and Clark had one major task to complete over the winter months. They had never planned to take the keelboat with them when they resumed the expedition in the spring. Rather, the plan was to load the boat with boxes of plant and animal specimens and other gifts and artifacts the expedition had picked up on the way. The seven enlisted men who were signed on only as far as Fort Mandan would take the keelboat down the river and eventually deliver it and its contents to President Jefferson in Washington.

To go with the boxes, Lewis and Clark also prepared a lengthy and detailed report to President Jefferson with descriptions of the conditions they had encountered, their observations of the stars, accounts of the animal and plant life, discussions of the various Indians, and journals including sketches of all that they had seen.

Lewis was a gifted and enthusiastic naturalist, and it was often he who collected the samples and made sketches of the plants and animals they saw. Many animals were previously unknown to him, such as the badger, coyote, prong-horned antelope, and the prairie dog, which was found throughout the prairie living in a network of tunnels. Lewis shot and preserved animals when he could. If not, a sketch would do, along with a brief essay describing the animal down to the measurements of its body parts. For plants, Lewis noted where each

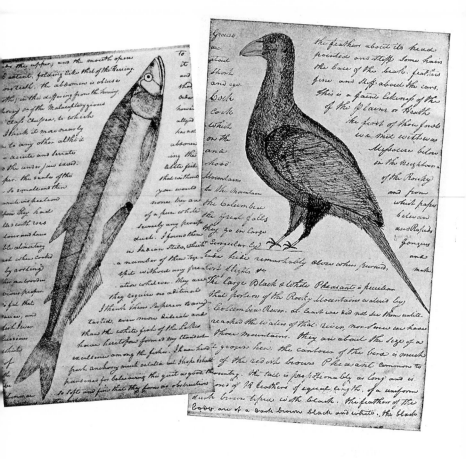

Lewis included many sketches in his journal of the animals the Corps encountered, such as these drawings of a fish and a bird.

had been found, how and when it grew, and whether the plant might be useful to medicine.

Clark was a naturally talented mapmaker, and he kept measurements of the river and surrounding land, and drew beautifully detailed maps from his

Dated April 7, 1805, this is the first page of the letter from Lewis to President Jefferson from Fort Mandan. Included with this letter was an inventory of all the animals, plant specimens, and artifacts gathered by the Corps to send back to Jefferson.

findings. A good deal of what they would be sending to Washington—the specimens, the accounts of the Indian tribes, the maps—was completely new information. Lewis thought President Jefferson would be very pleased with the scientific, geographical, and cultural knowledge they had gained.

The intellectual activity was a nice change from the daily physical work, as the men also spent hours upon hours trying to free their boats from the river, where they were completely iced in. As Clark describes in his journal, it was a difficult task made worse by weather so cold that "Lewis took off the Toes of one foot of the Boiy who got frostbit . . ." In December and January, the temperature usually rose only a few degrees above zero during the day. The ice on the river had become so thick it could hold the weight of crossing buffalo herds. Using everything from axes to boiling water, the men worked for days to release the boats. The cold weather also brought the nighttime event known as the northern lights, a spectacular appearance of rippling colored light in the sky.

Though by and large it was a peaceful and productive winter, there were some disturbances. The Hidatsa planned several raids on neighboring tribes, in spite of the Corps' objections. One of the expedition's main objectives was not only to befriend the Indians, but to encourage them to make peace among themselves. But there were longstanding feuds and arguments between tribes.

In 1834, Karl Bodmer painted this portrait of Mandan Chief Mató-Tópe, whose name means "Four Bears." Mató-Tópe's clothing is typical of a Mandan chief's.

A band of Sioux and Arikara attacked a Mandan hunting party and stole several horses. Lewis and Clark met with the Mandan chiefs and made suggestions to them about how to respond, but their suggestions were not taken. The relationships between the various Indian tribes of the Missouri River were extremely complicated. No matter how good their intentions, Lewis and Clark could not understand these tribal relationships after only a few months in the area. Life simply went on.

The coming of spring was a huge relief after the bitter winter. Clark noted "all the party in high Sperits they pass but fiew nights without amuseing themselves dancing . . ." The Mandan were used to these frigid winters and had almost superhuman resistance to the cold. But the men of the Corps had suffered from rheumatism and frostbite, and had good reason to be so cheerful at the arrival of warmer weather.

In March, when the ice on the Missouri River began to break up, it was almost time to move on.

Chapter Five

We saw also many tracks of the white bear of enormous size . . . we have not as yet seen one of these anamals, tho their tracks are so abundant and recent. the men as well as ourselves are anxious to meet with some of these bear. the Indians give a very formidable account of the strength and ferocity of this anamal, which they never dare to attack but in parties of six eight or ten persons; and are even then frequently defeated with the loss of one or more of their party.

JOURNAL OF WILLIAM CLARK, APRIL 13, 1805

I find that the curiossity of our party is pretty well satisfyed with rispect to this anamal.

JOURNAL OF MERIWETHER LEWIS, MAY 6, 1805

*A*fter the long months of doing very little but hunting and making new canoes, the men were quite ready to start the expedition again. They had come sixteen hundred miles already, and figured they had two thousand more to go before reaching the Pacific Ocean. Their winter quarters were in

Very little information is available about what Sacagawea looked like. All paintings of her, including this portrait by the artist E. S. Paxson, are imagined likenesses.

today's state of North Dakota. Their route would now begin to curve west to the Upper Missouri in what is now Montana.

Also preparing for the journey were the trader Charbonneau, his wife, Sacagawea, and their now two-month-old baby, Jean Baptiste. After spending the winter with Charbonneau, neither Lewis nor

Clark had the feeling he would be a particularly valuable addition to the Corps. His translation skills were not all that good, and his character was less than admirable. But Sacagawea might be the key to their success, and so her husband was made welcome.

There was a great deal of anticipation surrounding the expedition's departure. So far, they had been traveling through lands that trappers and traders had visited before them. Now, to their knowledge, they were about to cross into territory that no white man had ever seen. On every map Lewis had studied, this vast region appeared as a blank space. It was up to the Corps of Discovery to fill in those blank areas.

It was an exciting prospect. As Lewis put it in his journal on April 7, "we were now about to penetrate a country at least two thousand miles in width, on which the foot of civilized man had never trodden . . . I could but esteem this moment of departure as among the most happy of my life."

As they neared the area where the Missouri

and Yellowstone rivers meet, they passed through a beautiful prairie and into a marshy area thick with shrubs. They encountered hard winds that blew heavy waves against their boats and slowed them down, but there were plentiful herds of buffalo and elk on land, and the animals had no fear of the humans. One buffalo calf even became affectionately attached to Lewis, trotting after him as he took a walk on the banks.

They began to see the famed grizzly bears (they called them white bears), which they had heard so much about from the Mandan. At first the men were confident of their ability to kill grizzlies, thinking that the Indians with their bows and arrows were simply underarmed. But after several encounters with the massive animals, they quickly understood that the strength and deadly force possessed by these bears should not be underestimated.

One group chanced upon a bear almost nine feet tall, which they had wounded earlier in that day. The furious animal attacked the six men, whose combined gunshots did not take the bear down.

An illustration from Patrick Gass's journal shows Captain Clark and his men shooting at the grizzly bears, which proved to be formidable antagonists.

Because their rifles could fire only one shot each before needing to be reloaded, the men had no choice but to run. It was not until the bear had chased several of the men into the river and was beginning to swim after them that a shot from a man on shore finally killed it.

In mid-May, in present-day Montana, the expedition's progress was interrupted by another near-disaster. The fast current and brisk winds turned one of the pirogues onto its side, dumping its contents into the river. The expedition's most precious cargo—the detailed maps, journals, and drawings documenting every discovery—began to float away. To the frustration of the others, Charbonneau panicked at his place by the rudder and did not respond to the shouted directions of the other men. It was Sacagawea, most likely with her tiny son on her back, who saved the day by gathering up the books and papers as they floated by.

Many historians agree that the role of Sacagawea has often been exaggerated and romanticized. This in no way, however, takes away from the importance of what she did contribute. From the viewpoint of history, saving the expedition journals could be her greatest contribution. But if asked, the men in the Corps of Discovery might have felt that her knowledge of local roots and berries was more important. She gathered such tidbits as wild artichokes and turnips, which added variety to the Corps' meals and greatly improved the food's flavor.

Lewis continued his habit of exploring the land on foot and collecting plant and animal samples while the boats sailed or were towed along the river, which had now turned to head almost directly west. It was on one of these walks, on May 26, that he caught a glimpse of mountains in the distance. Even farther beyond those mountains lay the Rocky Mountains—the greatest obstacle between the Corps and the Pacific Ocean.

From the little they had been told by the Mandan and Hidatsa, Lewis and Clark had the optimistic idea that with the help of horses, the Rockies could be crossed in a day or less. In fact, the range is enormous, since the Rockies extend from Canada in the north to Mexico in the south. Some of the mountains that separate Montana from Idaho measure more than nine thousand feet high. But the full height of the mountain range was not yet apparent to Lewis at a distance. Nonetheless, as he wrote in his journal that evening, he was beginning to realize the "difficulties which this snowey barrier would most probably throw in my way to the Pacific."

The men were captivated by the changing landscape, which now bore magnificent chalk-covered cliffs and bluffs and oddly shaped outcroppings. The constant flow of water running down the cliffs over thousands of years had fashioned the rock into strange sculptures. Lewis variously described them as looking like "lofty freestone buildings," "statuary," "Long galleries," and "ruins of eligant buildings." It was near this area that Clark named the Judith River, after a young lady that he hoped to marry after returning home.

The direction of their route, for the first time, was unclear. Up to this point, following the Missouri River had been relatively straightforward. But now they were in virtually unknown territory, and on June 2 they came to an unexpected fork in the river. The Mandan had not mentioned a major river splitting from the Missouri in this spot, and Sacagawea, unfamiliar with this particular area, could not advise them. In a place now called Decision Point, the expedition came to a halt, to deliberate over which fork was the true Missouri.

The north fork was muddy, and the south fork clear. Both Lewis and Clark guessed that since the Missouri was supposed to run down from the mountains, the water should be clear. Although this convinced them that the south fork was probably the correct route, they explored the north fork as well. If they were to reach and cross the mountains before the autumn, time was of the essence. They could not afford to be anything less than absolutely certain.

They took almost a week to hike and take measurements, Lewis and his party scouting the north fork, and Clark and his party the south fork. After comparing their findings, Lewis and Clark still both believed the south fork to be the correct route of the Missouri. Almost every man in the Corps disagreed. However, because they had such trust in their two leaders, the men accepted the decision to take the south fork in spite of their misgivings.

From the information the Indians had given them, Lewis now expected to come upon an enormous waterfall. The sound of the pounding water reached his ears before the falls were in sight. Shortly thereafter he saw sprays of water high in the air. There was no mistaking it—they were approaching the Great Falls of the Missouri. When the falls themselves finally came into view, the sight was heart stopping. In his journal, Lewis declared it "the finest sight I have ever beheld."

Over eighty feet high and nine hundred feet wide, the water of the Great Falls thundered down in a seething torrent of froth. The cascading water sounded like a herd of stampeding buffalo. The air was thick and cool with spray. The raging currents turned the water varying shades of blue, turquoise, and green. It was a powerful and unforgettable scene, and also meant good news. Here was positive proof that in choosing the south fork of the river, they had gone the right way and followed the true Missouri.

Their happiness dimmed, however, when Lewis set out on foot to explore the path around the falls. As he walked he was surprised to find a second, smaller waterfall above the first one. Then he

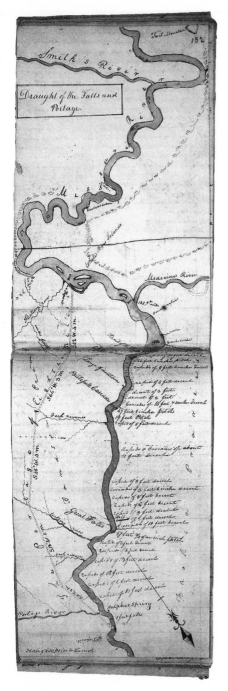

Smith's River

Draught of the Falls and Portage.

Medicine River

Great Falls

Portage River

found a third. A fourth.
And a fifth. Lewis had
planned to spend only a
day or two on the portage,
carrying the boats and supplies on land past the
waterfall. Now he found
they would have to portage
not one but *five* waterfalls,
a distance of over sixteen
miles. This would cause a
serious delay in reaching
the mountains. And it was
not their only problem.

Sacagawea had taken
sick, and now, at the Great
Falls, she appeared to be
dying.

Clark drew this map in 1805. It
illustrates the path the men took to
move their boats beyond the waterfalls.

Chapter Six

. . . the current excessively rapid and dificuelt to ascend
great numbers of dangerous places, and the fatigue
which we have to encounter is incretiatable the men
in the water from morning untill night hauling the cord
& boats walking on sharp rocks and round sliperery
stones which alternately cut their feet & throw them
down, notwith standing all this dificuelty they go with
great cheerfulness, added to those dificuelties the
rattlesnakes inumerable & require great caution to
prevent being bitten . . .

JOURNAL OF WILLIAM CLARK, JUNE 15, 1805

Sacagawea was delirious. She did not seem to
know where she was. She experienced strange
muscle spasms, and her pulse was terribly faint.
Though today it is believed she was suffering
from an inflammatory disease of the pelvis, Lewis
had no way to know what ailed her. Using guess-
work, he treated the young mother with a heated
compress of Peruvian bark, opium from his medical
supplies, and drinks of sulfur water from a spring.

Miraculously, Sacagawea began to regain her strength, and within several days she was feeling better. Lewis recorded, "She is free from pain clear of fever, her pulse regular, and eats as heartily as I am willing to permit . . . I think therefore that there is every rational hope of her recovery." This medical crisis behind him, Lewis could now focus his full attention on portaging around the waterfalls.

The portage was probably the most brutal and punishing labor the men had performed since the beginning of the expedition. They had built several crude wagons, on which they placed their boats. These were half dragged, half pushed over the rough terrain. Most of the supplies were taken by hand. It was hot, the mosquitoes were plentiful and aggressive, and the work was backbreaking. Perhaps the greatest causes of difficulty were the prickly pear plants that grew in unbelievable numbers along their path.

Members of the cactus family, prickly pears are fruit-bearing plants covered with stiff hairs and thorns. The men wore moccasins made from animal skins, and the prickly pear thorns easily cut through the soles. The path was also filled with sharp rocks and the ruts of bison track, which added to the foot wounds from the prickly pears. Most of the men were in agony. And because everything could not be carried at once, they had to retrace their steps to pick up additional supplies. All in all, they made four round-trip passages, taking a total of eleven days. If Lewis and Clark ever had a time to feel pride and good fortune in the endurance of their men, it was now.

Though the men worked through the Fourth of July, there was still an opportunity to celebrate in the evening. One of the men played popular tunes

The fifteen-star flag was the official flag of the United States at the time of the expedition. The one pictured here is the Star-Spangled Banner, the famous flag that inspired Francis Scott Key to write the national anthem.

on his fiddle. In spite of the exhausting work, the Corps was happy to honor Independence Day, its country's birthday.

When preparing for the expedition, Lewis knew it might be necessary to get a boat around an obstacle such as a waterfall. Because of this, he had designed a boat that could be collapsed in size so that it could be easily carried and assembled when needed. This would allow them to leave one of their larger boats behind, thus avoiding yet another portage.

When all the portages were finally completed, Lewis helped put together the collapsible boat he had brought, which would be used in place of a boat that had been left at the Great Falls. An animal skin was attached onto the iron frame of the boat and then dried in place over a small fire. Finally, the boat was sealed with a mixture of charcoal and beeswax.

Unfortunately, the boat leaked badly when tested and had to be left behind. Lewis was greatly disappointed in the failure of his vessel, and in his diary that night wrote, "I need not add that this circumstance mortifyed me not a little." To replace the leaky boat, the Corps made two new dugout canoes from local trees.

Lewis had never imagined losing so much time at the Great Falls, first during the portage and then building new boats. If they could not make up some time and cross the Rockies soon, they might not make it to the Pacific Ocean before the winter. The new canoes were not completed and river-ready until July 14. They were launched on July 15, and to Lewis's joy the Corps could now begin in earnest to look for the Shoshone.

By mid-July the evenings were getting cooler, and the expedition still had found no trace of the Indians. The river flowed into a gorge approaching the Rockies, a section Lewis named the Gates of the Rocky Mountains. The water here was rough and full of powerful currents. After the physical toll the portage had taken, the men were further broken down by their daily battles against the river. To make matters more difficult, game was no longer plentiful. There was meat to be found, and although no one was going hungry, it was clear that with the coming of fall, big game would be harder to find and kill. The dog, Seaman, was often helpful with smaller game. Lewis's journal notes that Seaman caught two geese on July 20, but they did not provide much meat.

Sacagawea was hopeful that her people could be found near the Three Forks area, where three smaller rivers formed the Missouri. Clark and some men went ahead on foot searching for Indians. On July 27, the Corps reunited at the Three Forks, naming the smaller rivers Jefferson, Madison, and Gallatin, after the president, secretary of state, and secretary of the treasury. By this time, Clark was exhausted and practically crippled by gashes in his feet made by prickly pears. Lewis noted in his journal that Clark was ill and had developed a fever.

After resting for several days, they went up the Jefferson River, with Lewis and Clark frequently taking separate parties to continue the search for the Shoshone. Surprisingly, neither Lewis nor Clark took Sacagawea with them on these forays. Since they held high hopes that she was the key to their establishing a good relationship with the Shoshone, their failure to include her is a mystery.

As they continued up the Jefferson, Sacagawea spotted a familiar landmark from her childhood, Beaverhead Rock. This was another sign that they were in Shoshone territory. The following day, August 9, Lewis and his three men set out on foot on another search, leaving Sacagawea behind with Clark and the main party. The landscape was beautiful, mostly flat plains with stunning mountain views in the distance. They hiked for several days without incident. Then on this grassland, seemingly out of nowhere, a mounted figure appeared several hundred feet away. Lewis immediately recognized him as a Shoshone Indian. But Lewis had not only left Sacagawea behind again, he had not even asked for some basic Shoshone phrases. The only word he had learned from her was *ta-ba-bone,* which he understood to mean "white man." In reality, to the Shoshone, it meant something closer to "stranger."

The Indian did not respond when Lewis called out the word. Here he was, face to face with a Shoshone, whose help he desperately needed to buy horses, and he was unable to communicate.

Lacking words, Lewis began to display the gifts he had brought as proof of his peaceful intentions. He put his gun on the ground to show he

Three Shoshone warriors are depicted in this 1861 painting by George Catlin.

posed no threat and signaled his men to stop. But one of them missed the signal and kept moving. Abruptly, the Shoshone wheeled his horse and cantered away, and the four men of the Corps were left standing alone. It was a bitter disappointment.

After camping out, Lewis and his men continued the search the next morning. They followed an Indian road that angled uphill toward a mountain ridge. Running alongside the road was a small stream, which grew more and more narrow as the path climbed. Lewis knew that this ridge was the location of the Continental Divide, the line that marks the division of eastward- and westward-flowing waters in North America. On one side of it, running water, from the smallest of streams to the greatest of rivers, flows toward the west. On the other side of the divide, they flow toward the east. The tiny stream in front of Lewis—easily crossed with a simple leap—was the very beginning of the great Missouri River itself.

It was a triumphant but sobering moment. When Lewis stood on the Continental Divide, he had a clearer view of the mountains they would have to cross. This portion of the Rockies is known as the Bitterroot Range. The mountains were significantly larger than Lewis had imagined, and even in August their summits were blanketed in snow. Clearly, the most difficult and dangerous part of their journey to the Pacific Coast still lay ahead.

Lewisia rediviva, which was named for Meriwether Lewis, is the state flower of Montana. The Corps discovered this plant, whose common name is bitterroot, in Montana.

In addition to his concern about the mountain crossing, Lewis also had to deal with another large disappointment. He could now see that there was obviously no all-water route linking the eastern continent with the Pacific Ocean. One of President Jefferson's primary goals for the Corps of Discovery had been to locate this Northwest Passage. Lewis would now have to report that the passage did not exist.

But there was no time to focus on his disappointment. The sight of the massive snow-covered mountains made it all the more plain that they had to make the crossing as soon as possible. The longer they waited, the colder and more difficult the conditions would be. They needed to leave immediately.

But first they had to find horses.

Chapter Seven

I have been wet and as cold in every part as I ever was in my life, indeed I was at one time fearfull my feet would freeze in the thin Mockirsons which I wore . . .

JOURNAL OF WILLIAM CLARK, SEPTEMBER 16, 1805

*T*he following day Lewis and his men came across a small group of Shoshone women collecting food. This time, things went more smoothly. Though one woman ran away, Lewis was able to approach two more. Had he not left Sacagawea behind with Clark, he could have communicated with the women easily. In any event, through hand gestures, he convinced them of his peaceful intentions. Since they had no way of defending themselves, the Shoshone women had little choice but to agree. They accepted the small gifts he offered, and by the time a much larger party of male warriors appeared nearby, things were quite friendly.

There were sixty Shoshone warriors now on the scene, all on horseback. It was very fortunate that Lewis had encountered the small group of women first. The warriors were suspicious and prepared to fight, but the women displayed the gifts they had received and insisted that these strangers were friendly.

Lewis and his companions were brought to the local chief, Cameahwait, and they shared a meal together. In the customary manner of his tribe, Cameahwait hugged Lewis and pressed his cheek to Lewis's face, until the explorer was covered with grease and war paint. All around the Shoshone village stood grazing horses—hundreds of them. Through sign language, Lewis managed to communicate the two crucial facts: There were more white men nearby, and they all needed to buy horses from the Shoshone to cross the Bitterroot Mountains. Cameahwait agreed to return with Lewis to meet the others.

In this painting by E. S. Paxson of Lewis and Clark's camp at Travelers' Rest, Clark and Sacagawea, holding her son, are seated on the right. In the center, George Drouillard introduces Lewis to three Salish Indians. Clark's slave, York, is standing to the left of Lewis.

When they reached the place they had agreed to meet up, however, Clark, his men, and Sacagawea were not there. Lewis spent a tense night waiting. In his journal, he explained that "my mind was in reality quite as gloomy all this evening as the most affrighted indian but I affected cheerfullness to keep the Indians so who were about me." With each passing hour, the Shoshone had more time to consider that perhaps Lewis was tricking them. He might be

in league with their enemies, the Blackfeet, and planning to attack them.

But by morning, Lewis spotted Clark, Sacagawea, and the main body of the Corps in their canoes on the river, heading toward them. In one of the canoes, Sacagawea turned to Clark and began rapidly signing to him that Lewis was with members of her tribe. Clark expected a joyful reunion to follow, but as Sacagawea climbed out of the canoe and approached the chief on shore, her behavior bewildered the explorers. She became very emotional, gesturing and bursting into tears all at once.

It took a while for the men in the Corps to sort out the source of her feelings. First, Sacagawea had recognized her old friend Jumping Fish, a girl who had been with her on the very day Sacagawea had been captured. But a greater revelation was that the chief, Cameahwait, was Sacagawea's brother! She had not seen him since the day the Hidatsa had carried her off as a young girl.

The Corps had more than their share of good fortune on the journey, and this perhaps was the luckiest stroke of all. It had been just a series of random events that resulted in Sacagawea joining the expedition. Now it turned out she was blood kin to the only man who could help Lewis and his men over the mountains. It is not surprising the site was later named Camp Fortunate.

The Shoshone were more than willing to trade their horses for goods. Though they had many horses, they were otherwise quite poor. Food was scarce, and they were frequently raided by the Blackfeet and other tribes. They traded their horses on very reasonable terms. Lewis was pleased with the results, writing that he personally "obtained three very good horses. for which I gave an uniform coat, a pair of legings, a few handkerchiefs, three knives and some other small articles the whole of which did not cost more than about 20$ in the U' States."

The terms of the trades, and the directions to the only passable area of the mountains, were conveyed in a complicated way. The Shoshone gave the information to Sacagawea, who translated it into Hidatsa, which her husband, Charbonneau, spoke. He then translated the information into French to yet another Corps member (as his English was very poor). The information was then given to Lewis and Clark in English. It was a time-consuming, but vital, process.

Once the translation chain had given the necessary information, everyone was in a hurry to get moving. The Corps was worried about the colder weather, and the Shoshone were eager to join other Shoshone tribes on a buffalo hunt. Twenty-nine horses were bought, and Lewis took on a guide they

Animal hides were used as clothing, and tribes often decorated them with paintings of scenes from everyday life, as seen in this Shoshone elk-hide painting of a buffalo hunt.

called Old Toby to show the Corps the correct route. They would be following the path used by the Nez Perce Indians, who lived on the plains west of the mountain range.

The expedition got under way again on September 1, after the men had buried some of their heavier belongings to be picked up on the return trip. It was difficult going for both men and horses. Most of the men did not ride but instead walked alongside the animals, which were carrying saddlebags packed full of heavy supplies. There was thick undergrowth and rocky ground, and the way was steep. Clark wrote that they struggled ". . . up & Down Steep hills, where Several horses fell, Some turned over, and others Sliped down Steep hill Sides . . ." To make matters worse, by the third day it had begun to snow.

They were in the west-central area of present-day Montana near the Idaho border, preparing to ascend and cross the Bitterroot Mountains on Lolo Pass. It was a heavily wooded area, cold, wet, and windy. There was very little game to be hunted. They had gotten some fresher horses from a tribe of Salish, or Flathead, Indians they had come upon, but even these horses were losing strength.

By mid-September they were moving up slopes so steep that the horses sometimes pitched over backward. Their estimate of a five-day crossing was now known to be far too optimistic. The path was overgrown. The men had too little food and too little strength. By the fifth day in the mountains, the Corps had to kill one of the younger horses for food. The day after that, a snowstorm began. Old Toby took a wrong turn, and they were lost for two days before refinding the path. By now, even Lewis was growing sick from lack of enough food and poor nutrition.

By September 16, the men were broken down and close to giving in to their hunger pangs and exhaustion. Eight inches of snow had fallen. Despite their best hunting efforts, no game could be found. Another horse had to be killed for food. Two days later, Clark and several others went ahead of the main party in the hopes of finding some better source of meat.

Several days behind Clark, Lewis finally reached a ridge and saw a wide, flat plain lying beyond it. It was a difficult descent, but with the knowledge that they would shortly be beyond the dreadful mountains, the men pressed on. As they descended, they found part of a horse that Clark had left behind for them to eat, along with a note saying that he was heading for the plains to hunt.

As Lewis led his group down the last, flattening path of the mountain, they were met by one of Clark's men, who brought some fish that Clark had gotten from the Nez Perce Indians on the plains. By nightfall, the entire Corps of Discovery was reunited in the Indian village, and at long last there was enough food to fill every stomach. Unfortunately, the effects of so much food on starving digestive systems were harsh. And the camas roots that were a big part of the Nez Perce diet did not sit well in their stomachs. Almost everyone became ill, with vomiting and diarrhea. The preferred treatment of Dr. Rush's "thunderbolt" pills only made the men sicker.

What they could not have known during this time, when almost every man was weakened by illness, was that the Nez Perce were deciding whether to kill them. From the Indians' viewpoint, there was no reason not to. Here was a group of men with weapons and supplies that the Nez Perce

A group of Nez Perce Indians meets a government surveyor near the Bitterroot River in Montana in this 1853 engraving.

desperately needed. They were strangers, they were weak, and they were unable to defend themselves. So far they had done nothing but eat the Indians' food. Why shouldn't the Indians simply do away with them and make themselves richer?

But one woman spoke up on the Corps' behalf. It was not Sacagawea, who probably knew nothing of the discussion. It was an old woman who had been captured long ago by the Blackfeet, and later lived with a group of white traders. She had now returned to live with her own people, and she readily told them that the white traders had been very good to her, unlike the Blackfeet. These white men were friends, she insisted, and must not be harmed. Her people listened and decided to help, not kill, the white men.

Clark brought a Nez Perce chief named Twisted Hair to meet Lewis. The three sat down and looked over a map that Twisted Hair had drawn on an elk skin, showing the details of the territory that lay ahead. By following the Clearwater and Snake rivers, they would come to the Columbia River, which led west toward the Pacific Ocean. If Twisted Hair's guess was right, they should reach the Columbia in one week.

The Corps branded their horses with markings that showed they belonged to Lewis and asked the Nez Perce to watch over them until their return. They made five new canoes in the Indian-dugout fashion, burning the wood, then hollowing it out. From here to the Pacific, they would, once again, be relying only on their boats for travel. Their route would take them from the Clearwater River and the Snake River in Idaho to the Columbia River, bordering present-day Washington and Oregon. On October 7, the Corps was on the move again.

Twisted Hair's map and time estimates proved to be quite accurate. He and a second Nez Perce chief had agreed to come along part of the way with the expedition to act as translators for any Indians they would come across.

The currents were swift and sometimes dangerous, but it was a welcome change. Every mile they had progressed up the Missouri River had been against the current. Sometimes it was a little tussle, and other times it was out-and-out warfare. Now, on the Clearwater, the current was at last working with them. Rather than battling against it, they rode its power down the river, letting it carry them closer and closer to the Pacific Ocean.

Chapter Eight

Great joy in camp we are in view of the Ocian, this great
Pacific Octean which we been so long anxious to See. and
the roreing or noise made by the waves brakeing on the
rockey Shores (as I suppose) may be heard distinctly . . .

JOURNAL OF WILLIAM CLARK, NOVEMBER 7, 1805

The dugouts were swept rapidly along the Clearwater River. There were occasional spills into the
water, but no one was seriously hurt. By now, most
of the men in the Corps were used to these river
mishaps. But their Shoshone guide, Old Toby, thor-
oughly alarmed by the rapids, left at the earliest
opportunity and headed back to his village.

The boats were coming to the Snake River,
and the men now often met Indians as they passed
their villages. With the help of Twisted Hair, these

This illustration from Patrick Gass's journal shows two men and a horse struggling after their canoe strikes a tree branch and is overturned.

meetings were friendly, and many of the Indians had food to sell.

When they reached the Columbia River on October 16, its banks were lined with Indians of the Wanapum and Yakima tribes. Here the Corps purchased a large quantity of a type of food that only Clark seemed to find unappetizing—dog meat. Even

Lewis, who was so fond of his own dog, Seaman, liked the taste of it. After getting by almost entirely on fish in recent weeks, the men were longing for any kind of red meat. The meat was a badly needed change to their diets. The waters of the Columbia that they were nearing would be the roughest they had yet come across.

The area of falls that the Corps was about to pass through was the territory of Indians who spoke a Chinookan language. Since these Indians were enemies of the Nez Perce, Twisted Hair and the other Nez Perce chief said their good-byes to Lewis and Clark and returned to their home. The Corps was without an Indian guide who knew the land (Sacagawea did not). They did, however, have a large audience of Indians watching as they took their dugouts over the falls known as the Dalles. When the Corps succeeded in negotiating the falls without loss of life or boat, the Indians were quite surprised.

On November 1, 1805, the expedition passed through a final series of rapids and falls, the

In this 1905 painting by Charles Russell, Sacagawea interprets Lewis and Clark's intentions for a group of Chinook Indians as they travel on the Columbia River.

Cascades, between what today is Washington state and Oregon. They continued to meet Indians almost every day and to buy goods from them. However, it seemed the closer they got to the Pacific Ocean, the higher the prices they were charged for the things they needed. These Indians had access to trade goods from ships and sailors on the Pacific Coast. The items the Corps had to offer were no longer considered unusual or sought-after. The men were also falling victim to some theft by the Chinook Indians—almost every day another small item went missing. Though they were getting closer and closer to the ocean, the mood in the Corps was growing grim.

They passed into a wooded area, cold, foggy, and uncomfortably damp, and Clark described the entire group as "wet and disagreeable." But the mood was joyful on November 7, when the men believed they had their first glimpse of the Pacific Ocean. Actually, they were seeing an estuary, a place where the river and ocean waters meet, but the ocean itself lay only twenty miles away. And its effects on the river were significant.

Even on a calm day, the enormous waves would have made controlling the dugouts difficult. But the waves were made much worse by terrible

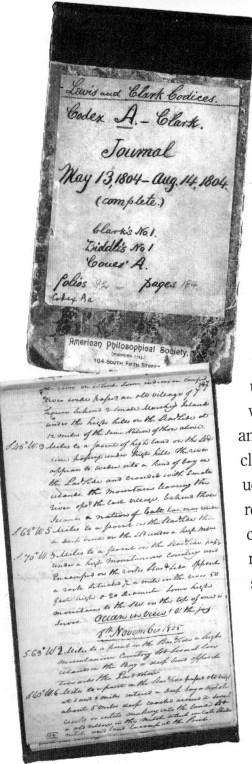

storms, with high winds, thunder, and lightning. Whether the men were struggling downriver or settled down in camps onshore, the conditions were miserable. Clark recorded that "the rain continues all day, we are all wet also our bedding and maney other articles." The storm continued for days without relief. At what is now called Point Ellice, they made camp and took shelter until November

The front cover and entries from one of William Clark's journals. The entry near the bottom of the journal page illustrates Clark's excitement on seeing what he thought was the Pacific Ocean: *"Ocian in View! O! the joy."*

15, when they were finally able to progress past the point.

Here was the ocean that had been their goal for so long. Clark wrote that "men appear much Satisfied with their trip beholding with estonishment the high waves dashing against the rocks & this emence Ocian." But reaching the ocean was not a completely joyful occasion. Taking scouting parties out along the coast, Lewis and Clark had a clear view, north and south, of the Pacific. They had hoped to find a ship here, or even a camp of sailors. This would have meant access to new supplies and the possibility of transport home by sea. Lewis had been given an unlimited letter of credit from President Jefferson, which would have allowed him to spend as much as he needed. But they found neither ships nor other white men.

They were disappointed, but they still had reason to feel extraordinary pride. They had just accomplished President Jefferson's dream. Though they had found that the Northwest Passage did not exist, they had crossed the continent to the Pacific

Ocean. They had discovered hundreds of new plant and animal species. They had made contact with many Indian tribes. And through their friendship with the Nez Perce and by crossing Oregon to the coast, they had taken the first step toward establishing an American presence in the territory west of the Rockies, land on which the United States currently had no claim.

Lewis and Clark at this point faced a choice. Should they set up camp on the north side of the Columbia River, or should they explore the south bank first? Though the decision was clearly Lewis and Clark's to make, they put the matter to a vote, and every member of the expedition had a say. It was certainly a minor event in the Corps of Discovery, and probably took only a few minutes to complete. But during those few minutes, another first in history had been achieved—included in the votes tallied were one cast by an Indian woman and one cast by a black slave. Through the eyes of history, it is a remarkable example of true democracy in action.

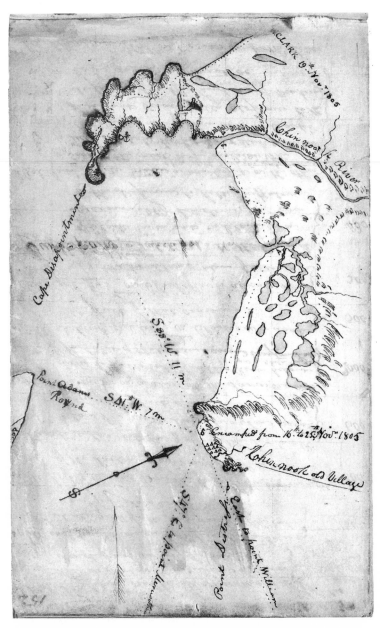

One of many drawn by Clark on his journey, this map from November 1805 shows Cape Disappointment in Washington state, near the mouth of the Columbia River.

The Corps chose a site on the south side of the Columbia in the forest, within walking distance of the beach. They built several small log cabins and called their new home Fort Clatsop. This was the territory of the Chinook and Clatsop tribes. Both were friendly and had furs and food to trade with the men. Since it was understood the expedition would be spending the winter in their camp, the need to rush was gone. The Corps had time to explore, to enjoy the strange sights and smells of the ocean, and to hunt for fresh meat.

The artist John Clymer called this 1974 painting *Sacagawea at the Big Water.*

There was plenty to keep the men's attention over the winter. They started a salt-making operation, keeping large fires burning to boil down ocean water for salt. In addition to hunting and exploring, they tanned hides and made leather from elks that they killed and used the hides to fashion new clothes, moccasins, and sleeping bags. Their old clothing and bedding was crumbling from a combination of heavy use and the wet conditions. Though it was a relief not to have to brave the bone-chilling temperatures they had faced during their winter with the Mandan, the cool, damp weather often made life just as uncomfortable. It was difficult to keep food fresh, and easy to get sick or develop skin boils. The camp also suffered from an infestation of fleas.

Clark kept himself quite busy during the winter months with his mapmaking. Before the Corps' arrival, no other white men had ever passed through the territory between the Mississippi River and the Pacific Ocean. Clark worked each day on his map. Once the last portion was done, it would be the first map in history to contain a detailed look at the continent west of the Rockies.

Meanwhile, Lewis created a highly descriptive work for President Jefferson that included everything from sketches of certain Indian canoes to essays on the appearance and habits of local wildlife. The information recorded at Fort Clatsop that winter would have a lasting effect for

A reconstruction of Fort Clatsop in Astoria, Oregon, is built on the site of the Corps' 1805–06 winter quarters.

naturalists, mapmakers, and politicians throughout the United States.

By the end of March 1806, it was time to pack up and start the return journey. For after their incredible achievement traveling more than four thousand miles across the continent, there could be no triumphant return to civilization without doing the exact same thing a second time. They would have to retrace their steps. But this time, there was no more experienced group of travelers in the world to make the trip.

The Corps had very few goods left to trade. Just enough, as it turned out, to obtain one canoe. Unable to reach terms with the Indians for the second canoe they needed, Lewis lost patience and had his men steal it. It was certainly not the best parting act, and it showed how their relationships with the Indian tribes had deteriorated since their friendships with the Mandan and Nez Perce. On March 23, having left a note in their cabin recording their presence and their expedition, the Corps set off for home.

The way was both familiar and difficult. They

were heading upriver now, against the powerful currents that had been so helpful on their journey west. They ran into trouble with the Chinook-speaking Indians as they portaged past the Cascades. Some of the Indians became hostile, and there were several incidents of attempted theft, including that of Lewis's dog. Three members of the Corps set out after the thieves and retrieved Seaman, but Lewis was greatly angered by the incident. The Corps' meeting with the Walla Walla, however, was very friendly, and the tribe proved to be gracious and generous hosts. They were as kind and honest as the Chinook-speaking Indians of the Cascades had become aggressive and thieving.

The Nez Perce also did not disappoint. As promised, they had kept the Corps' horses and promptly returned them. They provided what food they could, though hunting was bad and there was not much for anyone to eat. The Nez Perce also had news of the Lolo Pass—it was still deep with snow. Lewis had no choice but to remain in the Indian village and wait for the conditions to get better.

William Clark engraved his signature and the date July 25, 1806, into this rock. Now known as Pompeys Pillar National Monument, it is the only remaining physical evidence of the Lewis and Clark expedition in Montana.

Eager as the men were to get home, no one wanted to try another mountain crossing in the snow.

After one false start in June, and with the help of Nez Perce guides, they crossed the Bitterroot Mountains without much hardship. When they reached what is now Montana, the party split. Though they were all eager to return home, there were still some geographical questions Lewis and Clark wanted to answer.

Clark's party, including York, Sacagawea, and Charbonneau, began by retracing their steps east, collecting the supplies they had buried on the first trip. Lewis's party traveled on horseback along the Bitterroot and Blackfoot rivers to the Great Falls. For later expeditions, this created a shortcut that shaved hundreds of miles off the trail. At the Great Falls, the party split again. Lewis and three men went north to explore the Marias River area, while the remaining men stayed on the Missouri.

Lewis was now with only a small party of men in Blackfeet country, a tribe known to be hostile and very dangerous. Back at the Great Falls, Indians of an unidentified tribe had stolen seven horses during the night. Lewis was very eager to keep clear of the Blackfeet altogether, but this time an encounter could not be helped.

A group of eight mounted Blackfeet warriors spotted Lewis's party. Their presence no longer secret, Lewis took charge by approaching the Indians rather than trying to run. The two groups camped out together, communicating through sign language. At first Lewis thought his friendly overtures were being returned. But he was wrong.

On a trip to America in the 1830s, the Swiss artist Karl Bodmer created many detailed drawings and paintings of Indian life, including this portrait of a Blackfoot warrior on horseback.

At daybreak the next morning, Lewis awakened to find some of the Blackfeet in the process of stealing their guns and horses. Perhaps the Indians felt they were acting in their own defense, as Lewis had told them that his group were friends of the Nez Perce, who were longtime enemies of the Blackfeet. To the Blackfeet, this friendship meant the Nez Perce would now have access to guns of their own.

Whatever the motivation of the Blackfeet, it is quite possible they planned to kill Lewis and his men after taking the guns.

Lewis's men awakened just in time to stop the theft, and a fight broke out. When it was over, two of the Blackfeet were dead and six had fled. It was the only fatal violence between the Corps and Indians to occur on the expedition. Knowing they now risked being captured or killed by the angry Blackfeet, the men packed their belongings and raced all one hundred twenty miles back to the Missouri River. Some two weeks later, they reunited with Clark's party, and the Corps was complete again. They hastily headed downriver, out of Blackfeet territory.

The tinge of ill fortune remained for the rest of the journey home. Lewis was wounded when one of his own men accidentally shot him. Upon arriving at the Mandan villages, they had to say goodbye to Sacagawea, Charbonneau, and the child Jean Baptiste. Another man, Colter, elected to depart on a trapping expedition. The Corps did gain the

Corps member Hugh McNeal is chased up a tree during a close encounter with a grizzly bear. The illustration is from Patrick Gass's journal.

company of Sheheke, a Mandan chief who agreed to accompany them to Washington to meet the president. And though they did not stop, harsh words were exchanged from boat to shore with the Teton Sioux. This was an unfortunate reminder of one of the expedition's failures—they were not able to make friends with the Teton Sioux or the Blackfeet.

By now, they were passing through present-day Nebraska, making excellent progress with the help of the current. They began to encounter groups of traders heading upriver. It was September of 1806, and the Corps had been away from civilization for almost two and a half years. Lewis and Clark were eager for the news the traders provided, especially the news of President Jefferson's re-election. But the most entertaining news they heard was that of the Corps itself. The expedition was thought by many to be lost and probably dead. The latest story passed quickly from boat to boat—the men of the Corps of Discovery, having lost only Sergeant Floyd, were alive and well and making their way downriver!

Lewis and Clark finally came into view of St. Louis on September 23, just over twenty-eight months after they had left. Cheering people lined the riverbank and guns were fired in celebration as the expedition paddled into shore. With this welcome, the Corps returned from the unknown, and stepped into the pages of history.

Epilogue

Newspapers everywhere carried excited reports of the return of the Corps of Discovery. They were famous. They were heroes. They were honored wherever they went.

President Jefferson himself was thrilled with the success of the expedition. The news that the Northwest Passage did not exist was disappointing, but the huge number of discoveries more than made up for it. The men were awarded twice their agreed-upon pay by Congress, and each man also received three hundred twenty acres of land. For Lewis and

Clark, the land grant was sixteen hundred acres each.

Not long after returning home, Clark married his sweetheart, Judith. When their first son was born, Clark named him Meriwether Lewis Clark, a sign of the respect he held for his friend. Clark became a respected businessman, and the foster father to Charbonneau and Sacagawea's son, Jean Baptiste, who came to live with him for a time in St. Louis. At least nine years after the expedition, Clark granted York his freedom. From what we know, York went into business hauling supplies with the wagon and team Clark had given him, but the freed slave had great difficulties in the trade.

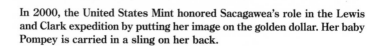

In 2000, the United States Mint honored Sacagawea's role in the Lewis and Clark expedition by putting her image on the golden dollar. Her baby Pompey is carried in a sling on her back.

The Lewis and Clark Centennial Exposition was held in Oregon in 1905 to celebrate the 100th anniversary of Lewis and Clark's extraordinary journey.

Though York is supposed to have died on his way to St. Louis, where he planned to see Clark, a trapper claims to have met York living out west among the Crow Indians many years later.

Unhappily, Lewis's life after the expedition was filled with difficulties. He was made governor of the Louisiana Territory, but life in government and a desk job did not suit his wandering nature. Before long he was in financial trouble, lonely, and drinking too much. The details of his new life seemed to overwhelm him. In 1809, probably suffering from depression, Lewis took his own life.

His accomplishments remain, however. Lewis and Clark's partnership resulted in some of the greatest exploration achievements in this country. Because of their loyal work, they provided a great gift to Americans both in their own time and in ours. Two hundred years later, we can look back through history and see America through the eyes of Lewis and Clark. It is the only glimpse we will ever have of the continent in its pure state, green and lush and alive with the possibilities to come.

Selected Bibliography

Ambrose, Stephen E. *Lewis & Clark: Voyage of Discovery.* Washington, DC: National Geographic Society, 1998.

Ambrose, Stephen E. *Undaunted Courage: Meriwether Lewis, Thomas Jefferson, and the Opening of the American West.* New York: Touchstone, 1997.

Barry, Louise. *The Beginning of the West.* Topeka, KS: Kansas State Historical Society, 1972.

Betts, Robert B. *In Search of York: The Slave Who Went to the Pacific with Lewis and Clark.* Boulder, CO: University Press of Colorado, 1985.

Blum, John M., Edmund S. Morgan, Willie Lee Rose, Arthur M. Schlesinger, Jr., Kenneth M. Stamp, and C. Vann Woodward, eds. *The National Experience: A History of the United States to 1877.* New York: Harcourt Brace Jovanovich, 1981.

Blumberg, Rhoda. *The Incredible Journey of Lewis & Clark.* New York: Scholastic, 1987.

Catlin, George. *Catlin's Letters and Notes on the North American Indians.* North Dighton, MA: JG Press, 1995.

De Voto, Bernard, ed. *The Journals of Lewis and Clark.* Boston: Mariner Books, 1997.

Duncan, Dayton, and Ken Burns. *Lewis & Clark: The Journey of the Corps of Discovery: An Illustrated History.* New York: Alfred A. Knopf, 1999.

Hunt, Norman Bancroft. *Native American Tribes.* Edison, NJ: Chartwell Books, 1997.

Lewis, Jon E. *The Mammoth Book of the West.* New York: Carroll & Graf Publishers, 1996.

Neider, Charles, ed. *The Great West: A Treasury of First-hand Accounts.* New York: Da Capo Press, 1997.

Schmidt, Thomas. *National Geographic Guide to the Lewis & Clark Trail.* Washington, DC: National Geographic Society, 1998.

Schmidt, Thomas, and Jeremy Schmidt. *The Saga of Lewis & Clark: Into the Uncharted West.* New York: DK Publishing, 1999.

Wexler, Alan. *Atlas of Westward Expansion.* New York: Facts on File, 1995.

Photo Credits

Index